To my wife, Emily. Thank you for making me a "dog guy" and a better person.
—JJ

For Lucky and all the rescued souls, this book is filled with love!
—WT

Text © 2024 by Jack Jokinen
Illustrations © 2024 by Wendy Tan
Cover and internal design © 2024 by Sourcebooks

Sourcebooks and the colophon are registered trademarks of Sourcebooks.

This artwork was created in Photoshop using a display tablet.

Published by Sourcebooks eXplore, an imprint of Sourcebooks Kids
P.O. Box 4410, Naperville, Illinois 60567-4410
(630) 961-3900
sourcebookskids.com

Cataloging-in-Publication Data is on file with the Library of Congress.

Source of Production: 1010 Printing Asia Limited, Kwun Tong, Hong Kong, China
Date of Production: March 2024
Run Number: 5034935

Printed and bound in China.
OGP 10 9 8 7 6 5 4 3 2 1

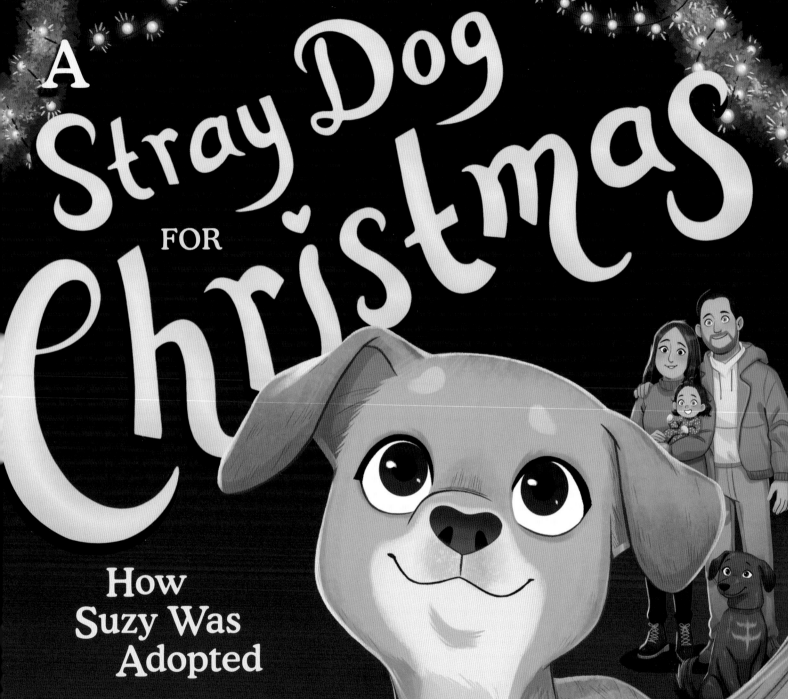

A Stray Dog for Christmas

FOR

Christmas

How
Suzy Was
Adopted

Words by
JACK JOKINEN

Pictures by
WENDY TAN

sourcebooks
eXplore

It was two weeks before Christmas,
on a cold winter's night.

A stray dog wandered the streets alone.

She didn't yet have a name, but she would soon be called Suzy.

The snowflakes blew in circles. The ground froze beneath her paws. Her stomach growled. Suzy looked up and down the street, but all she saw was a blanket of snow.

I need somewhere warm to spend the night, Suzy thought with a shiver.

So she walked...

and walked...

and walked.

Finally, Suzy saw a light.
A soft, welcoming light.

It shined through an open
door to a lovely house.

WELCOME

She peeked inside,
and her little heart
skipped a beat.

The house smelled like cinnamon and pine cones. Warm air wrapped around her face, tickling her whiskers and inviting her in.

It's comfy and cozy
in here, Suzy thought.
I'll just rest my head
for a little while.

Soon, she was curled
up, fast asleep.

Outside, a neighbor noticed the open front door.

"How strange," he said. He reached in and closed the door.

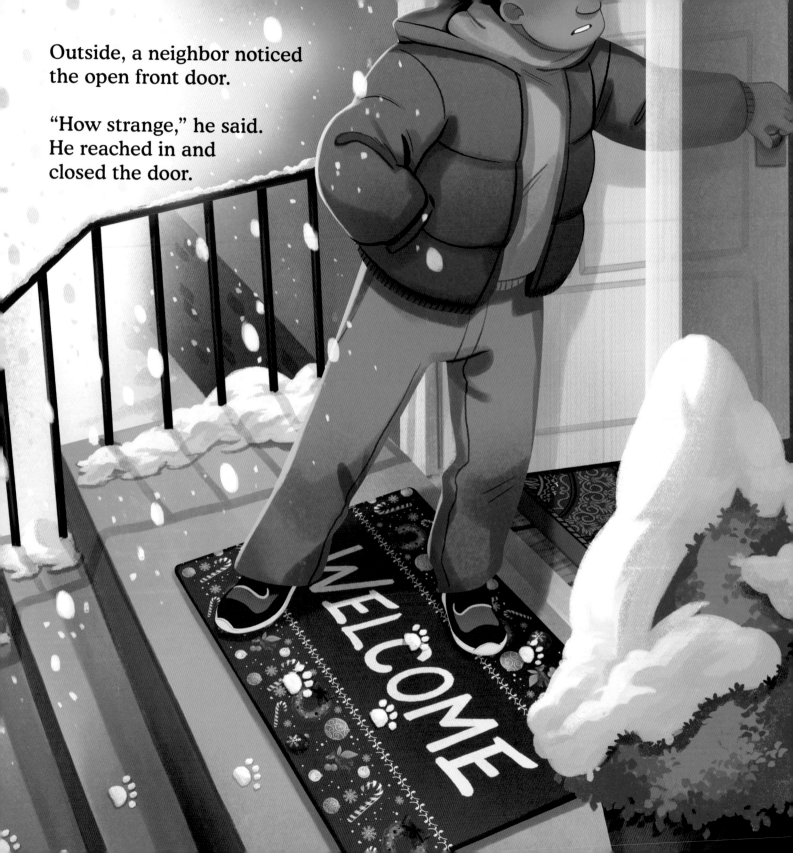

The neighbor did not know it,
but he had shut Suzy inside.

When morning came,
a woman entered the
living room.

"Ah! There's a dog in our
house," she gasped.

"How on earth did you get in here?" she asked.

Suzy slowly leaned forward and wondered,
Will she like me?
Will she be my friend?

That's when the woman ran upstairs, shouting,
"Jack, there's a dog in our house!"

"Of course, there is, Emily," said Jack. "His name is
George, and he's a very good boy."

"No, silly. Not our dog," Emily cried.
"There's another dog in our house,
and she's on the stairs."

Confused, Jack jumped out of bed
and ran to take a look.

There was Suzy, staring up at him
with her big brown eyes.

"What?

   How?

When?

   Why?"

Jack asked.

But Suzy didn't bark or move.

She studied the man with the funny look on his face.
She wondered, *Will he like me? Will he be my friend?*

Just then, Suzy's stomach rumbled.

Jack leaned over her and said, "You poor thing. You're all skin and bones. Let's get you some food."

Food? Her ears perked up.

While Jack grabbed a bowl, Suzy wiggled her butt and wagged her tail.

The food tasted better than anything she could remember. She gobbled it up happily until her hunger went away.

When Suzy looked up, she was shocked to see the other dog, George, who had poked his head into the kitchen.

Suzy looked at him. He looked back at her.
Suzy wondered if George was friendly like Emily and Jack.

She wondered,
Will he like me?
Will he be my friend?

Suzy glanced back at Jack and Emily. She looked around the house at the twinkling lights and bright decorations. Then she peeked out the window at the cold, snowy city.

Suzy didn't want to be outside and alone again. She wanted to stay with the family inside the house that smelled like cinnamon and pine cones.

So Suzy did something brave.
She took a step forward and
kissed George on the nose!

George tilted his head. He took a deep breath. Then gave her a sniff and a lick.

"Oh, they like each other!" Emily said, clapping her hands.

Jack bent down and proudly patted both dogs on their heads.

Suzy sat up a little taller and wagged her tail hard. *I hope I never have to leave*, she thought.

Well, Suzy *did* have to leave the house,
but only to see a doctor to make sure she
wasn't hurt. The doctor gave her some medicine and
said she would be all better with food, rest, and lots of love.

Suzy was so happy, she purred like a cat.

They love me! she thought. *And I love them.*

Emily turned to Jack.
"You know she is ours now, right?"

"I know," said Jack, smiling.
"And she'll need a name.
She looks like a Suzy to me!"

So Suzy became part of the family. She had a bed to sleep on and a bowl full of food.

George became
her furry brother.

She even gained
a baby sister,
Johanna.

Suzy would never have to be alone again.

She had found her
forever home.

Author's Note

When Suzy came through our door in December 2019, another dog was the last thing our family needed. With a one-month-old baby and a dog already, we could have dropped Suzy off at a shelter and hoped she would find a loving home. But that would've been the easy decision. The right thing is not always the easy thing, and I've always prided myself on doing what is right. When I looked down at Suzy's sweet face, I knew the only choice was to welcome her as a part of our family. She may not have survived in a shelter, and I couldn't stand the thought of that if we could help her. So we did.

As Suzy settled into our home, there were countless vet appointments, several accidents in the house, and multiple pairs of chewed-up sneakers. It has taken a lot of love and patience to care for her,

but seeing Suzy get a new shot at life, and watching our daughters, Johanna and Layla, (we've had another baby girl!) grow up with her has made it all worth it.

Also, thanks to our story going viral, many people decided to help us with Suzy's medical bills. The donations poured in, far exceeding the amount we needed for Suzy. As her health improved, we were faced with other tough questions: What do we do with the excess money? Do we keep it for Suzy? Do we give it away, and if so, where to?

We decided to sponsor animal adoptions, offering $100 to help offset the cost of an adoption fee if someone rescued a dog instead of buying one. The results were incredible. During Suzy's first year with us, we sponsored three hundred and sixty-six adoptions, saving a life a day for the whole year!

It would have been the easy thing to simply give the excess donations to an organization, or even easier to keep the money for ourselves. But the right thing was to keep spreading Suzy's story to help other stray dogs like her find their forever homes.

When my two beautiful daughters grow up, I hope they look back on their childhood and are proud of their parents' choices. I hope this story inspires others to take the road less traveled and, when at a crossroads, choose to do what is right instead of what is easy. I hope you can do that too! It is so much more rewarding in the end.

Adopt, don't shop!

Before

& After